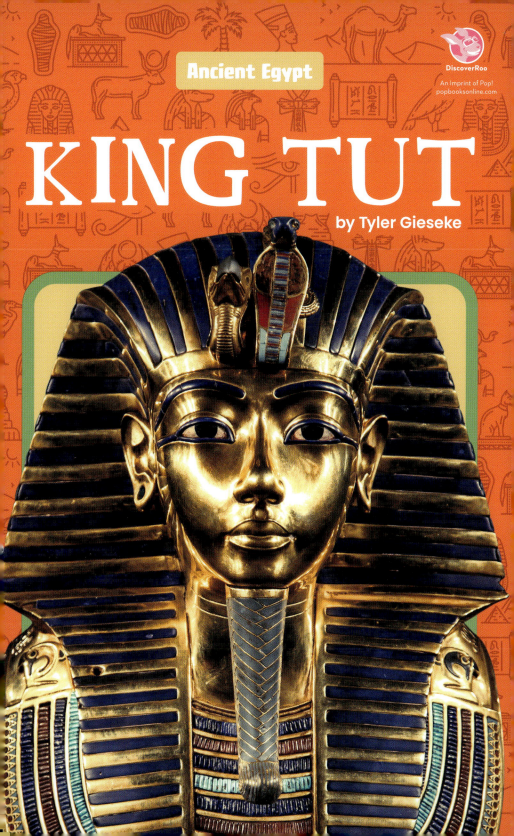

**Ancient Egypt**

# KING TUT

by Tyler Gieseke

abdobooks.com

Published by Pop!, a division of ABDO, PO Box 398166, Minneapolis, Minnesota 55425. Copyright ©2022 by Abdo Consulting Group, Inc. International copyrights reserved in all countries. No part of this book may be reproduced in any form without written permission from the publisher. DiscoverRoo™ is a trademark and logo of Pop!.

Printed in the United States of America, North Mankato, Minnesota.

052021
092021

Cover Photos: Jaroslav Moravcik / Shutterstock.com; Shutterstock Images

Interior Photos: Jaroslav Moravcik / Shutterstock.com, 1, 20–21, 29; Shutterstock Images, 5–6, 11–12, 23; iStockphoto, 8–9; Heritage Image Partnership Ltd / Alamy Stock Photo, 14; Associated Press, 17, 26; Gianni Dagli Orti/Shutterstock, 18; Mike Nelson/EPA/Shutterstock, 25; Mitzo / Shutterstock.com, 27

Editor: Elizabeth Andrews
Series Designer: Laura Graphenteen

Library of Congress Control Number: 2020948873
Publisher's Cataloging-in-Publication Data
Names: Gieseke, Tyler, author.
Title: King Tut / by Tyler Gieseke.
Description: Minneapolis, Minnesota : Pop!, 2022 | Series: Ancient Egypt | Includes online resources and index.
Identifiers: ISBN 9781532169915 (lib. bdg.) | ISBN 9781644945377 (pbk.) | ISBN 9781098240844 (ebook)
Subjects: LCSH: Tutankhamen, King of Egypt--Juvenile literature. | Rulers of the ancient world--Juvenile literature. | Egypt--Civilization--To 332 B.C.--Juvenile literature. | Egypt--History--Juvenile literature.
Classification: DDC 932.01--dc23

# WELCOME TO DiscoverRoo!

Pop open this book and you'll find QR codes loaded with information, so you can learn even more!

Scan this code* and others like it while you read, or visit the website below to make this book pop!

## popbooksonline.com/king-tut

*Scanning QR codes requires a web-enabled smart device with a QR code reader app and a camera.

# TABLE OF CONTENTS

**CHAPTER 1**
The Boy King . . . . . . . . . . . . . . . . . . . 4

**CHAPTER 2**
One God or Many?. . . . . . . . . . . . . . 10

**CHAPTER 3**
A Great Discovery . . . . . . . . . . . . . . .16

**CHAPTER 4**
Clues and Questions . . . . . . . . . . 24

Making Connections. . . . . . . . . . . . 30
Glossary . . . . . . . . . . . . . . . . . . . . . . .31
Index. . . . . . . . . . . . . . . . . . . . . . . . . 32
Online Resources . . . . . . . . . . . . . . 32

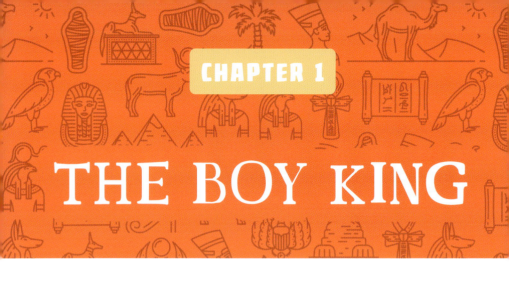

# CHAPTER 1

# THE BOY KING

An Egyptian boy walks along the Nile River. It is 1333 BCE. He listens as a royal helper talks to him.

The boy's name is Tutankhaten, or Tut for short. He is only nine. Yet, he has many duties. He is Egypt's newest **pharaoh**!

WATCH A VIDEO HERE!

*Ancient art shows King Tut and his wife when they are older.*

Tut's father, Akhenaten, died a few years ago. Now, it's Tut's turn to rule.

*The Nile River overflows each year. This makes the soil along it good for plants.*

There is a lot of work to do. Akhenaten made big changes when he was pharaoh. But many Egyptian people are not happy with them.

One thing Akhenaten changed was the Egyptian religion. Egyptians had **worshipped** many gods for about 1,500 years. Akhenaten made people worship just one god instead.

He also changed the capital city. It used to be Thebes, in the south. Akhenaten moved it north to Amarna. But powerful people lived in Thebes. It had been the capital for many years.

**DID YOU KNOW?** Akhenaten ruled Egypt for 17 years, from 1353 to 1336 BCE.

As King Tut continues his walk along the Nile, he thinks about all this. He lifts his face toward the noon sun.

Tut imagines how he will make Egyptians happy again in the coming years. He knows what he has to do.

But he doesn't know what will happen long after he is gone. In about 3,000 years, people around the world will know Tut's name. They will recognize the face of the boy king. Tut's future **tomb** and all its treasures will display the wealth of ancient Egypt.

*Egyptians buried King Tut in a gold coffin.*

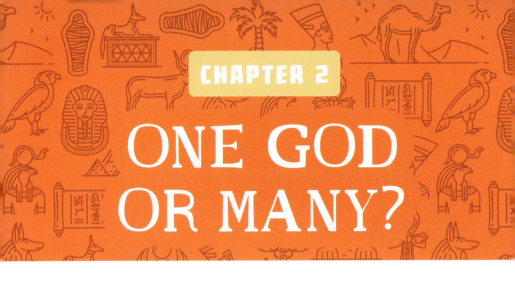

# CHAPTER 2
# ONE GOD OR MANY?

Ancient Egyptians **worshipped** many gods and goddesses. These powerful beings ruled over parts of nature. There were hundreds of them.

LEARN MORE HERE!

*Some Egyptian goddesses and gods had the heads of animals. Others had human heads.*

This wasn't true when Akhenaten was **pharaoh**. He changed the religion so that it had only one god, the sun god Aten. But Egyptians loved their old gods and goddesses. Many didn't want to give them up.

# TO AMARNA AND BACK

Thebes was the capital city several times during ancient Egyptian history. Amarna was the capital only once, for about 15 years.

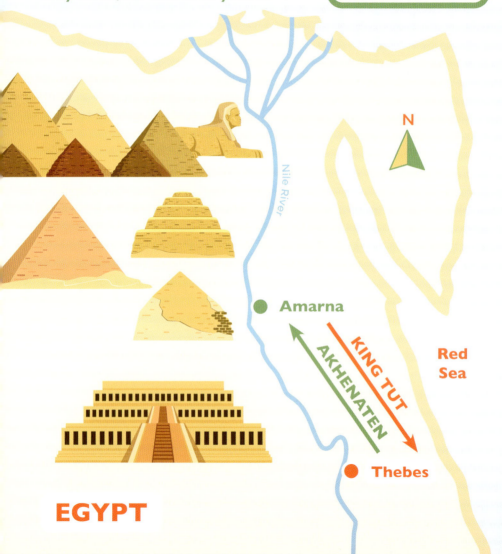

Tutankhaten tried to prove he was different from his father. He moved the capital city away from Amarna and back to Thebes. He also brought back the old goddesses and gods. He built **monuments** to them.

Tut even changed his name. Tutankhaten meant "living image of Aten," the sun god. His new name was "Tutankhamon," or "living image of Amon." Amon was the chief god of Thebes.

**DID YOU KNOW?** Amon could appear as a man or a ram. He was also connected to the sun god Re.

13

*This box from Tut's tomb displays his name in hieroglyphs, or Egyptian picture writing.*

Despite these steps, people put their anger at Akhenaten onto Tut. Later pharaohs almost succeeded in removing Tut from history.

Tut died when he was just 19. Then, people took his name off many things. Tut's name faded away. But 3,000 years later, his **tomb** made him famous again.

> ### HATSHEPSUT
>
> **Tut wasn't the only pharaoh Egyptians erased from history. Hatshepsut was one of just a few female pharaohs. She ruled from 1473 to 1458 BCE. She said she would rule until her stepson was old enough. But she ruled longer than that. After she died, her stepson had her name removed from buildings.**

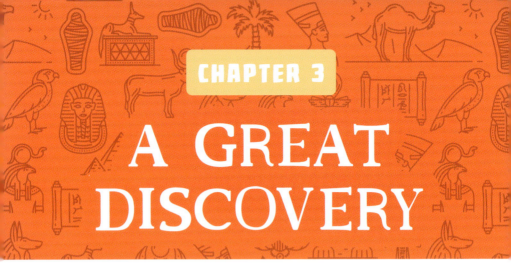

# CHAPTER 3
# A GREAT DISCOVERY

After about eight years of searching, **archaeologist** Howard Carter and his team reached Tut's **tomb** door in 1922. They were in the Valley of the Kings, near the ancient city of Thebes. Many **pharaohs** had tombs there.

COMPLETE AN ACTIVITY HERE!

*This 1922 photo shows the steps leading to King Tut's tomb.*

*Tut's belongings may have looked like this when Carter discovered the tomb.*

Carter carefully broke a hole in the door they found. When he looked inside, he saw the glitter of gold everywhere.

Riches filled the tomb of King Tutankhamon. Carter's team found more than 5,000 things inside. These included a royal seat, vases, and chariots. With so many items, it took ten years to take everything out of the tomb.

**DID YOU KNOW?** The Valley of the Queens is just south of the Valley of the Kings.

Three **coffins** covered Tut's **mummy**. The smallest one was made of solid gold! A gold mask on the mummy showed the young pharaoh's face. Later, museums around the world displayed the mask.

*King Tut's outer stone coffin*

# DIG DEEPER
# WITH KING TUT

## THE MASK AND ITS MEANING

The mask that was on King Tut's **mummy** is a very precious object. It is made of expensive materials, and its different parts have important meanings. It is on display in the Egyptian Museum in Cairo. The mask is known all over the world.

**Eyes** — Lines on the edge made of lapis lazuli, a favorite gemstone of Egyptians

**Face** — Covered in a combination of gold and silver

**Fake Beard** — A sign the **pharaoh** was **divine**

**Headdress** — Blue stripes made of glass

**Horus** — The god of pharaohs

**Vulture and Cobra** — Show the pharaoh ruled over all Egypt

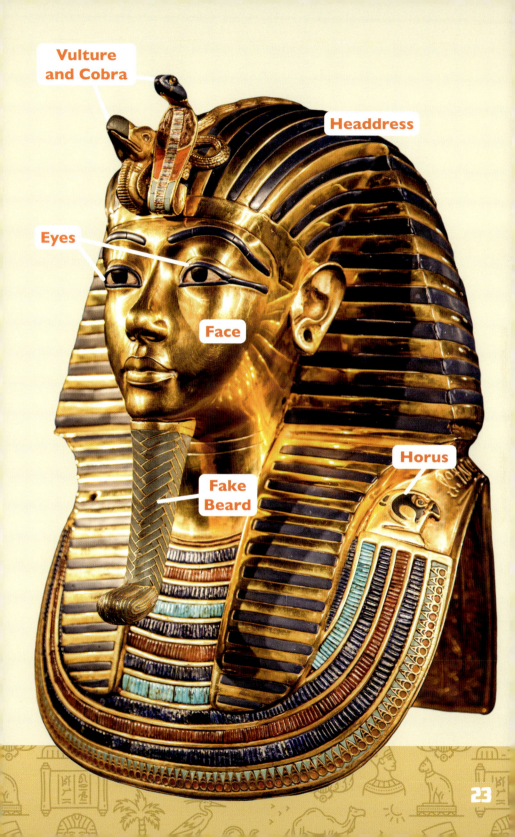

# CHAPTER 4
# CLUES AND QUESTIONS

The discovery of King Tut's **tomb** told scientists much about his life. In 2008, scientists studied Tut's bones. They discovered he had **malaria**.

LEARN MORE HERE!

*King Tut's mummy is intact even after more than 3,000 years in a tomb.*

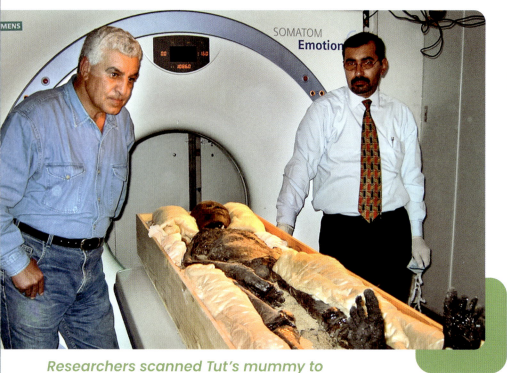

*Researchers scanned Tut's mummy to learn more about it.*

Tut's **mummy** showed he had a broken leg. Because of malaria, the leg might not have healed well. This problem could have led to Tut's death. But scientists don't know exactly how he died.

**DID YOU KNOW?** Scientists identified the mummies of Tut's mother and father in 2010.

*King Tut's tomb held six chariots.*

The discoveries have provided both answers and more questions about the boy king. There is still much to learn about King Tut. Even after studying his mummy and treasures, we can never know exactly what it was like to be **pharaoh** of Egypt at nine years old.

> **DID YOU KNOW?** Usually, Egyptians left the heart in a mummy when burying it. But Tut's heart hasn't been found!

*Tut's legacy will continue to inspire people.*

# MAKING CONNECTIONS

### TEXT-TO-SELF

How would you feel if you were the pharaoh at nine years old? Would you make the same decisions Tut did? Why or why not?

### TEXT-TO-TEXT

Have you read other books about ancient objects? How were those books similar to and different from this one?

### TEXT-TO-WORLD

Why do you think people are so interested in King Tut and his tomb? Is it important to know about people who lived long ago? Why or why not?

# GLOSSARY

**archaeologist** — a scientist who studies past human societies through the things left behind.

**coffin** — a container to bury a dead body in.

**divine** — having to do with or being a goddess or god.

**malaria** — an illness that causes fever and chills and is spread by mosquitoes.

**monument** — a building or statue made in honor of a person or event.

**mummy** — a dead body that is prepared so it doesn't break down like normal.

**pharaoh** — the highest ruler in ancient Egypt.

**tomb** — a place where people bury or put their dead, usually to honor them.

**worship** — to give praise and honor to a god or goddess.

# INDEX

Akhenaten, 5–7, 11–13, 27
Amarna, 7, 12–13
Carter, Howard, 16, 19
malaria, 24, 26
mask, 20, 22

name, 4, 9, 13, 15
Nile River, 4, 8, 12
religion, 7, 10–11, 13, 22
Thebes, 7, 12–13, 16
tomb, 9, 15–16, 19, 24

## ONLINE RESOURCES
## popbooksonline.com

Scan this code* and others like it while you read, or visit the website below to make this book pop!

## popbooksonline.com/king-tut

*Scanning QR codes requires a web-enabled smart device with a QR code reader app and a camera.